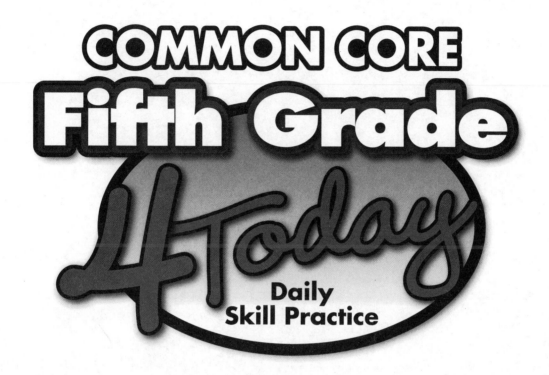

COMMON CORE
Fifth Grade
4 Today
Daily Skill Practice

Grade 5

Carson-Dellosa Publishing, LLC
Greensboro, North Carolina

Credits

Content Editors: Elise Craver, Christine Schwab, Angela Triplett
Proofreader: Josh Rosenberg

 Visit *carsondellosa.com* for correlations to Common Core, state, national, and Canadian provincial standards.

Carson-Dellosa Publishing, LLC
PO Box 35665
Greensboro, NC 27425 USA
carsondellosa.com

ISBN 978-1-4838-1239-7
01-213141151

Table of Contents

Introduction

Common Core Fifth Grade 4 Today is a perfect supplement to the fifth-grade classroom curriculum. Students' skills will grow as they support their knowledge of math, language arts, science, and social studies with a variety of engaging activities.

This book covers 40 weeks of daily practice. Each day will provide students with cross-curricular content practice. During the course of four days, students complete questions and activities in math, language arts, science, and social studies in about 10 minutes. On the fifth day of each week, students complete a writing assessment that corresponds with one of the week's activities.

Various skills and concepts in math and English language arts are reinforced throughout the book through activities that align to the Common Core State Standards. The standards covered for the whole week are noted at the bottom of that week's assessment page. For an overview of the standards covered, please see the Common Core State Standards Alignment Matrix on pages 5–8.

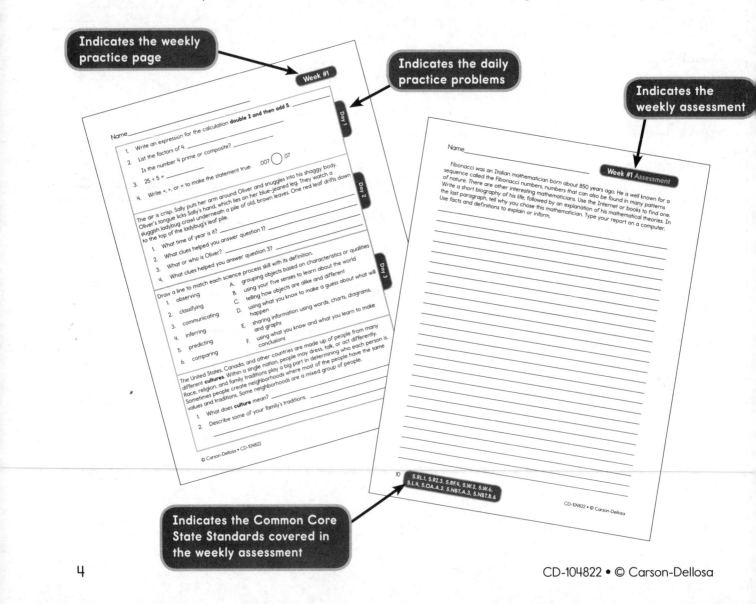

Indicates the weekly practice page

Indicates the daily practice problems

Indicates the weekly assessment

Indicates the Common Core State Standards covered in the weekly assessment

Language Arts

STANDARD	W1	W2	W3	W4	W5	W6	W7	W8	W9	W10	W11	W12	W13	W14	W15	W16	W17	W18	W19	W20
5.RL.1	●		●		●		●		●	●										
5.RL.2						●														
5.RL.3				●	●															
5.RL.4							●		●											
5.RL.5																				
5.RL.6											●									
5.RL.7																				
5.RL.9																				
5.RL.10																				
5.RI.1					●					●		●	●	●	●	●	●	●	●	●
5.RI.2									●				●				●			
5.RI.3	●						●	●						●			●			
5.RI.4		●	●	●	●						●	●			●		●	●	●	
5.RI.5																				
5.RI.6																				
5.RI.7																	●			
5.RI.8												●		●	●					
5.RI.9																				
5.RI.10				●									●	●	●	●	●	●	●	●
5.RF.3									●									●		
5.RF.4	●	●	●		●				●		●	●					●	●		
5.W.1						●								●						
5.W.2	●	●	●				●		●	●			●		●			●		
5.W.3				●	●	●		●			●	●				●	●		●	●
5.W.4		●			●		●		●		●	●	●						●	
5.W.5			●		●		●	●	●		●	●						●	●	
5.W.6	●							●						●		●				
5.W.7															●					
5.W.8						●	●	●		●			●		●		●			●
5.W.9																				
5.W.10			●	●											●			●	●	
5.SL.1																				
5.SL.2																				
5.SL.3																				
5.SL.4																				
5.SL.5																				
5.SL.6																				
5.L.1		●							●									●		●
5.L.2		●							●									●		●
5.L.3											●									
5.L.4	●				●				●		●	●								
5.L.5			●	●		●	●	●		●	●		●		●		●		●	
5.L.6		●	●	●	●	●	●	●	●	●			●		●		●	●		

W = Week

Language Arts

STANDARD	W21	W22	W23	W24	W25	W26	W27	W28	W29	W30	W31	W32	W33	W34	W35	W36	W37	W38	W39	W40
5.RL.1																	•	•	•	•
5.RL.2																				
5.RL.3																				
5.RL.4																	•	•		•
5.RL.5																				
5.RL.6																	•			
5.RL.7																				
5.RL.9																				
5.RL.10																				
5.RI.1	•	•		•	•	•	•	•	•		•	•	•	•	•	•		•	•	•
5.RI.2	•													•						
5.RI.3	•	•				•			•		•	•								
5.RI.4				•					•	•			•	•			•	•	•	
5.RI.5																•				
5.RI.6		•																		
5.RI.7												•								
5.RI.8	•																			
5.RI.9																				
5.RI.10	•	•	•	•	•	•	•				•	•	•		•					
5.RF.3														•		•	•		•	
5.RF.4	•				•	•	•	•		•			•	•		•	•			•
5.W.1				•	•	•		•	•	•				•				•		•
5.W.2			•			•	•			•			•	•	•		•	•	•	
5.W.3	•	•						•			•	•				•	•			
5.W.4				•			•	•		•	•			•						
5.W.5		•							•	•	•							•		•
5.W.6				•																
5.W.7			•											•		•				
5.W.8			•		•	•				•			•	•	•		•	•	•	
5.W.9																				
5.W.10		•																•		
5.SL.1								•							•	•				
5.SL.2																				
5.SL.3																				
5.SL.4																				
5.SL.5	•										•									
5.SL.6																				
5.L.1			•					•		•		•			•					
5.L.2			•					•		•		•			•					
5.L.3																				
5.L.4	•									•										•
5.L.5				•		•	•	•								•	•	•		•
5.L.6	•		•	•		•			•	•				•			•			

W = Week

CD-104822 • © Carson-Dellosa

Common Core State Standards Alignment Matrix

Math

STANDARD	W1	W2	W3	W4	W5	W6	W7	W8	W9	W10	W11	W12	W13	W14	W15	W16	W17	W18	W19	W20
5.OA.A.1										●							●			
5.OA.A.2	●		●					●	●			●		●						
5.OA.B.3			●				●						●						●	
5.NBT.A.1																●		●		
5.NBT.A.2				●						●					●					
5.NBT.A.3	●	●				●					●	●		●			●	●		●
5.NBT.A.4				●	●	●		●	●								●			
5.NBT.B.5					●					●						●		●		
5.NBT.B.6	●										●	●			●					
5.NBT.B.7		●			●	●			●					●		●				●
5.NF.A.1			●	●		●		●		●										
5.NF.A.2																		●		
5.NF.B.3												●		●						●
5.NF.B.4											●				●	●	●			
5.NF.B.5																				
5.NF.B.6																				
5.NF.B.7																				
5.MD.A.1																				
5.MD.B.2																				
5.MD.C.3																				
5.MD.C.4																				
5.MD.C.5																				
5.G.A.1																				
5.G.A.2																				
5.G.B.3																				
5.G.B.4																				

W = Week

Math

STANDARD	W21	W22	W23	W24	W25	W26	W27	W28	W29	W30	W31	W32	W33	W34	W35	W36	W37	W38	W39	W40
5.OA.A.1	•		•	•			•								•					
5.OA.A.2		•						•												
5.OA.B.3																				
5.NBT.A.1		•					•			•										
5.NBT.A.2														•						•
5.NBT.A.3			•		•			•					•	•		•			•	
5.NBT.A.4				•				•				•								
5.NBT.B.5											•	•								
5.NBT.B.6				•					•				•				•	•		
5.NBT.B.7		•				•				•										•
5.NF.A.1						•	•			•						•			•	
5.NF.A.2																				
5.NF.B.3																				
5.NF.B.4			•			•							•	•	•					
5.NF.B.5																				
5.NF.B.6																				
5.NF.B.7					•											•				
5.MD.A.1	•		•							•							•			
5.MD.B.2	•				•				•											
5.MD.C.3																				
5.MD.C.4		•		•																
5.MD.C.5						•	•	•					•		•		•	•	•	
5.G.A.1											•									
5.G.A.2															•			•		•
5.G.B.3													•							
5.G.B.4																				

W = Week

Name_____

---

1. Write an expression for the calculation **double 2 and then add 5**. _____

2. List the factors of 4. _____

   Is the number 4 prime or composite? _____

3. $25 \div 5 =$ _____

4. Write **<**, **>**, or **=** to make the statement true.   .007 $\bigcirc$ .07

The air is crisp. Sally puts her arm around Oliver and snuggles into his shaggy body. Oliver's tongue licks Sally's hand, which lies on her blue-jeaned leg. They watch a sluggish ladybug crawl underneath a pile of old, brown leaves. One red leaf drifts down to the top of the ladybug's leaf pile.

1. What time of year is it? _____

2. What clues helped you answer question 1? _____

3. What or who is Oliver? _____

4. What clues helped you answer question 3? _____

Draw a line to match each science process skill with its definition.

1. observing
2. classifying
3. communicating
4. inferring
5. predicting
6. comparing

A. grouping objects based on characteristics or qualities

B. using your five senses to learn about the world

C. telling how objects are alike and different

D. using what you know to make a guess about what will happen

E. sharing information using words, charts, diagrams, and graphs

F. using what you know and what you learn to make conclusions

---

The United States, Canada, and other countries are made up of people from many different **cultures**. Within a single nation, people may dress, talk, or act differently. Race, religion, and family traditions play a big part in determining who each person is. Sometimes people create neighborhoods where most of the people have the same values and traditions. Some neighborhoods are a mixed group of people.

1. What does **culture** mean? _____

2. Describe some of your family's traditions. _____

_____

Fibonacci was an Italian mathematician born about 850 years ago. He is well known for a sequence called the Fibonacci numbers, numbers that can also be found in many patterns of nature. There are other interesting mathematicians. Use the Internet or books to find one. Write a short biography of his life, followed by an explanation of his mathematical theories. In the last paragraph, tell why you chose this mathematician. Type your report on a computer. Use facts and definitions to explain or inform.

_____

_____

_____

_____

_____

_____

_____

_____

_____

_____

_____

_____

_____

_____

_____

_____

_____

_____

_____

_____

5.RL.1, 5.RI.3, 5.RF.4, 5.W.2, 5.W.6, 5.L.4, 5.OA.A.2, 5.NBT.A.3, 5.NBT.B.6

1. Write **<**, **>**, or **=** to make the statement true.   10.05 ◯ 10.005

2. Write 900,000 + 80,000 + 500 + 7 in standard form. _____

3. Start at 92. Create a pattern that adds 13 to each number.
    Stop after 5 numbers. _____

4. Emma spent $6.25 for spaghetti and meatballs, $1.12 for a bottle of water,
    and $3.75 for a piece of cake. How much money did Emma spend on her
    entire dinner? _____

Day 1

Correct the errors in each sentence.

1. Today, dad and i are going to the Park.

2. Its the Great Junkyard Racecar Day!

3. The fifth graders racecars had to be built using junk.

4. I can't weight to see whose racing first!

Day 2

1. What measurement system is used in the science community?

    _____

2. Why do all scientists use this system?

    _____

    _____

    _____

Day 3

The world **population** is more than seven billion. That's a lot of people! The number
is growing. In fact, about 250,000 people are born every day. These countries have
the most people, in order of largest population: China, India, United States, Indonesia,
Brazil, Pakistan, Bangladesh, Nigeria, Russia, and Japan.

1. Write the numeral that represents seven billion. _____

2. What does **population** mean? _____

3. What is one benefit about living in a place with a high population? _____

    _____

Day 4

Name_____

Have you ever been to a car, go-cart, or boat race? If you have, you know that racing vehicles have their own unique designs. The designs are carefully planned and include chosen colors and symbols. Vehicles also have numbers on their sides for identification purposes. If you were to design your own racecar, go-cart, or boat, what would it look like? What colors would you use? Choose your own number and explain your choice. Add an illustration. To organize your report, use paragraphs to separate topics.

_____

_____

_____

_____

_____

_____

_____

_____

_____

_____

_____

_____

_____

_____

_____

_____

5.RI.4, 5.RF.4, 5.W.2, 5.W.4, 5.L.1, 5.L.2, 5.L.6, 5.NBT.A.3, 5.NBT.B.7

Day 1

1. Write an expression for the calculation **triple 4 and then add 7 times 7**.

   _____

2. $(4 + 6) \div (9 - 4) =$ _____

3. $\frac{9}{10} + \frac{2}{5} =$ _____

Day 2

This story continues through Week 6.
A crow found a piece of cheese on the ground. She quickly swooped down to pick up the food and perched on a limb to enjoy the tasty treat. A fox wandered by and saw this.

1. This is one of Aesop's fables. What is a fable?

   A. a funny story   B. a true story   C. a story that teaches a lesson

2. What does the title tell us about the characters? _____

3. Are the animals personified in the first paragraph? Explain. _____
   _____

4. What was the first thing the crow did after grabbing the cheese? _____
   _____

Day 3

Write **true** or **false**. Rewrite any false statements to make them true.

1. _____ An experiment always tests a hypothesis.

2. _____ A scientist makes a prediction based on the results of the experiment.

3. _____ Experiments need to be controlled to make sure they are fair.

4. _____ It is important to change at least two variables during an experiment.

5. _____ All data needs to be carefully recorded during an experiment.

Day 4

Indigenous people are native to a particular region. Indigenous groups live all over the world. They may live in a desert, rainforest, frozen tundra, or the Australian outback. Some well-known North American indigenous groups are Apache, Hopi, Navajo, and Inuit. Indigenous people usually have their own traditions, dress, religious beliefs, and foods. They often share certain physical traits.

1. What does **indigenous** mean? _____

2. Choose an indigenous group and tell what you know.

   _____

Eggs sink in regular water. What can you do to make them float? Think about it. Write a report about any ideas you have for making eggs float. Describe what steps to take to experiment with your ideas. List any materials you might need. State what you think the outcomes will be. Later, use your ideas to try to make an egg float. Then, revise your report to include what you learned. Show your report to a teacher or another student. Make changes if needed.

_____

_____

_____

_____

_____

_____

_____

_____

_____

_____

_____

_____

_____

_____

_____

_____

_____

_____

_____

_____

_____

 5.RL.1, 5.RI.4, 5.RF.4, 5.W.2, 5.W.5, 5.W.10, 5.L.5, 5.L.6, 5.OA.A.2, 5.OA.B.3, 5.NF.A.1

CD-104822 • © Carson-Dellosa

Day 1

1. $400 \div 10^3 =$ _____

2. Lisa earned $31 each week delivering newspapers. She delivered newspapers for 2 weeks. How much money did Lisa earn after 2 weeks? _____

3. Round 7.38 to the nearest tenth. _____

4. $\frac{2}{3} - \frac{1}{6} =$ _____

Day 2

This story began on Week 3.
"Good afternoon, Crow," the fox called out politely. "How lovely you look today! I bet your voice is just as beautiful and that you sing the sweetest of all of the birds in the forest."

1. What compliment did the fox pay the crow? _____

2. What does a crow sound like? _____

3. Why do you think the fox said nice things to the crow? _____

4. During what time of day does this fable take place? _____

Day 3

Drew is experimenting on a circuit. He wants to know if the size of the wire used affects battery life. Identify the variables in Drew's experiment.

1. independent variable _____

2. dependent variable _____

3. controlled variables _____

_____

Day 4

There are many kinds of family **structures**. Some families are composed of a mother, father, and children. Some children live with just one parent. Other children may live with grandparents or other relatives. Some children live with their parents but frequently visit aunts, uncles, cousins, or grandparents. In some countries, extended family members live together in one home.

1. Write a synonym for **structure**. _____

2. Give examples of extended family members. _____

3. Who is in your immediate family? _____

   Think about your own family structure. Who lives in your home? Are you an only child or do you have siblings? How many generations of your family do you know or know about? On a separate sheet of paper, draw a simple family tree, starting with the oldest relative you know about. Then, write a report describing what you know about your family structure and history. Use paragraphs and headings to group your information. Share your first draft with a family member. Make changes if needed.

_____

_____

_____

_____

_____

_____

_____

_____

_____

_____

_____

_____

_____

_____

_____

_____

_____

_____

_____

_____

_____

_____

5.RL.3, 5.RI.4, 5.RI.10, 5.W.3, 5.W.10, 5.L.5, 5.L.6, 5.NBT.A.2, 5.NBT.A.4, 5.NF.A.1   CD-104822 • © Carson-Dellosa

1. Owen's bedroom has a perimeter of 46 feet. If the length of the bedroom is 11 feet, what is the width of the bedroom? _____

2. $309 \times 9 =$ _____

3. $50 \times 10^4 =$ _____

4. Tripp ran 4.8 times as many laps as Tony. If Tony ran 3.7 laps, how many laps did Tripp run? _____

This story began on Week 3.
The crow began to feel proud as she listened to the fox. She puffed up her feathers, lifted her beak into the air, and opened her mouth to show the fox her musical voice. Then, the cheese fell out of her mouth and tumbled to the ground. The fox grabbed the cheese and hungrily devoured it.

1. Why did the crow drop the cheese? _____

2. Do you think the fox meant those compliments? Explain. _____

3. What was the first thing the fox did after grabbing the cheese? _____

4. What clues tell you that the fox was probably hungrier than the crow? _____
_____

Scientists base their conclusions only on **empirical** evidence. Empirical evidence is based on facts and is objective, or free from opinions and biases. Write **E** for each empirical piece of evidence. Write **S** for each subjective piece of evidence.

1. __E__ The liquid maintained a temperature of 20°C.

2. __E__ Fourteen of the 30 pill bugs ate sample A.

3. __S__ The dogs that wore scented collars were better behaved.

4. __S__ The clothes washed in detergent C were the cleanest.

5. __E__ Using a shorter wire in the circuit had no effect on the volume of the buzzer.

The Anasazi tribe came to the southwestern United States around 100 BC. They built simple homes of sticks and mud in shallow caves among canyon walls. Later, they built more **sophisticated** apartment-style homes of adobe, sometimes four or five stories high. Suddenly, about 12 centuries later, all the pueblos were abandoned. No one knows where the Anasazi went, or why.

1. What does **sophisticated** mean? _____

2. What do you think might have happened to the Anasazi? _____
_____

Name_____

Lake Placid, Florida, is called a mural town because of all the murals painted on the outside walls of buildings around the town. Imagine that your mayor declares your town a mural town. She asks its citizens to paint murals on as many buildings as possible. You are a chosen artist and must paint one of the outside walls of your home or apartment building. How large will your mural be if it takes up an entire wall? What will you paint? Describe the scene. Show your essay to your teacher. Make changes if necessary. Include an illustration of your proposed mural.

_____

_____

_____

_____

_____

_____

_____

_____

_____

_____

_____

_____

_____

_____

_____

_____

_____

_____

1. Write **<**, **>**, or **=** to make the statement true.   101.05 $\bigcirc$ 101.005

2. $1\frac{3}{4} - \frac{7}{10} =$ _____

3. Gavin's anemometer measures the wind speed at 44.14 kilometers per hour, 4 times faster than the wind speed 5 hours ago. What was the wind speed 5 hours ago? _____

4. Round 7.2199 to the nearest thousandth. _____

Day 1

This story began on Week 3.
The fox smiled slyly. As he walked away, he called back to the crow, "It is not wise to trust those who praise you with many compliments."

1. Restate the fox's message in your own words. _____

2. What was the fox's message?
   A. Always compliment others.   B. Beware of false compliments.

3. Has anyone ever complimented you to get you to do something he wanted? If so, did it work? _____

4. Have you ever complimented someone to get what you wanted? If so, did it work? _____

Day 2

Write a word to correctly complete each sentence.

1. _____ is anything that has mass and takes up space.

2. The _____ is the building block of matter.

3. The smallest particle of matter is the _____ .

4. The _____ table lists all of the elements.

5. A _____ is a group of atoms bonded together.

Day 3

Egyptians, American Indians, and other ancient cultures drew pictures to tell stories. These pictures are called pictographs. Early Egyptian picture characters, as seen inside pyramids, are called hieroglyphs. American Indian picture characters, found on rocks and cliff sides, are called petroglyphs.

1. Draw a pictograph to symbolize something important to you. Then, explain.

_____

_____

_____

Day 4

Name_____

"The Fox and the Crow" is one of Aesop's Fables. Aesop was a Greek storyteller who lived more than 2,000 years ago. All of his fables were stories that taught a lesson. Use the Internet or books to read another of Aesop's Fables. Take notes as you read. Then, write a book report about the story. Describe the main characters. In the last paragraph, tell what you think Aesop intended for his readers to learn from the story. Do you agree with his position? Explain.

_____

_____

_____

_____

_____

_____

_____

_____

_____

_____

_____

_____

_____

_____

_____

_____

_____

_____

_____

_____

_____

_____

5.RL.2, 5.W.1, 5.W.3, 5.W.8, 5.L.4, 5.L.5, 5.L.6, 5.NBT.A.3, 5.NBT.A.4, 5.NBT.B.7, 5.NF.A.1

Day 1

1. Complete the table.

2. Complete the graph based on the table.

	Add 2	Add 3
1	3	4
2		
3		
4		
5		
6		

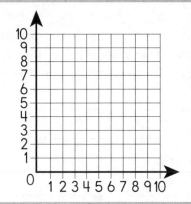

Day 2

I love water sports, especially waterskiing. That's why I invited my best friend, Andrew, over to give it a try. Andrew had never been on waterskis before, but he was a good athlete. So, I thought waterskiing would be a **breeze** for him. On his first try, Andrew let go of the tow rope as soon as the boat started to move. He sank like an anchor.

1. What do you know about Andrew? _____

2. What does the word **breeze** mean in this sentence? _____

3. Underline the clues that suggest that waterskiing might not be a breeze for Andrew.

4. What simile does the author use to describe Andrew? _____

_____

Day 3

1. How is a mixture the same as and different from a solution?

_____

_____

_____

2. Is salt water a mixture or a solution? Explain.

_____

_____

Day 4

Our calendar started with the year 1 AD, then 2 AD, and so on up to now, more than 2,000 years later. The year before 1 AD was 1 BC, and the numbers went backward from there.

1. Look at the time line. Fill in the square on the right side with today's year. Add your birth year. Add the years when Abe Lincoln was president (1861–1865), when the Revolutionary War started (1775), and when Egyptians built the pyramids (2500 BC).

| **1 AD** | | |

776 BC First Olympic Games

Write about the difference between a mixture and a solution. Give at least four examples of each. Then, name three methods anyone can use to separate a mixture. Use the Internet or books if you need more information. Include a T-chart listing examples of mixtures and solutions. Read your report to a classmate. Make changes if needed.

_____
_____
_____
_____
_____
_____
_____
_____
_____
_____
_____
_____
_____
_____
_____
_____
_____

1. $6\frac{3}{4} - 2\frac{3}{12} =$ _____

2. Round 4.769 to the nearest hundredth. _____

3. What kinds of lines are shown?

   _____

4. Write an expression for the calculation **double the number 6 and then subtract 36 divided by 12**. _____

Correct the errors in each sentence.

1. Wow, Mrs. nguyen's Kindergarten class is at the race too.

2. Is that you're sister over they're?

3. It looks like theyre making repairs to the cars front end.

4. That's becuz the car is going to fall a part.

1. Use the words in the word bank to help you explain the diagram.

| atoms | compound | molecule |

   _____

   _____

   _____

In 1807, the first successful steamboat puffed its way up the Hudson River in New York. Most people who traveled then did so by foot, horseback, wagon, or coach. In 1869, the Transcontinental Railroad was completed, making the first cross-country train travel possible. This also made rural mail delivery possible for the first time. In 1908, Henry Ford's Model T car was made available to the public.

1. Which verb is an example of onomatopoeia? _____

2. How did the invention of a widely available car change the world?

   _____

   _____

Think about how things have changed since you were born. Write an essay about the changes from past to present. First, look at the ways in which you have grown. Consider all the things you have learned to do since then. Finally, consider the world around you, including your own family or local or world news. List the changes you recall in proper sequence. Divide your essay into paragraphs separating topics. Type it on a computer. Then, show your essay to someone in your family. Make changes if needed.

_____
_____
_____
_____
_____
_____
_____
_____
_____
_____
_____
_____
_____
_____
_____
_____
_____
_____
_____
_____
_____
_____
_____
_____

5.RI.3, 5.W.3, 5.W.5, 5.W.6, 5.W.8, 5.L.1, 5.L.2, 5.L.5, 5.L.6, 5.OA.A.2, 5.NBT.A.4, 5.NF.A.1

Day 1

1. Round 33.01 to the nearest tenth. _____

2. 638.07 – 19.34 = _____

3. How many of each angle are in this shape?

   acute _____   obtuse _____   right _____

4. Write an expression for the calculation **subtract 9 from double 14**.

   _____

Day 2

Molly's family was busy preparing for dinner when Amy arrived. Molly directed Amy through the living room to the kitchen, which was filled with many **good smells**. Molly and Amy set the table. They gave each person a pair of chopsticks, a soup bowl, a soup spoon, and a rice bowl on a saucer.

1. Which word rhymes with **busy**: **Susy** or **dizzy**? _____

2. Which word would best replace **good smells**: **aromas** or **odors**? _____

3. How many individual items do the girls set at each place? _____

4. Predict whether or not Amy will enjoy the food. Underline the clues that helped you. _____

Day 3

1. What is friction?

   _____

   _____

2. Your class is discussing reducing friction. Name three ways to reduce friction.

   _____

   _____

Day 4

Long ago, people cleaned their teeth in interesting ways. The Egyptians made a tooth powder of ox-hoof ashes, myrrh, burnt eggshells, and pumice. Others scratched their teeth with a stick, wiped them with a rag, or chewed on crushed bones or shells. Tooth care has come a long way in the past few hundred years. Now, we use fluoride toothpaste, dental floss, and specially angled toothbrushes.

1. What did the tooth powder consist of? _____

   _____

2. What is the main idea of this passage? _____

   _____

3. Underline a word in the passage that has four syllables.

Math skills are important and not only for helping you pass a test. It is nearly impossible to go through a single day without doing something that requires a math skill. One example is how we pay for things. We count out change. We know the value of coins and add them up. There are many other ways we use math skills in our daily lives. Write an essay about why it is important to have math skills. Describe the many ways you use them. Ask two other students to read your essay and provide feedback. Make changes if needed.

_____

_____

_____

_____

_____

_____

_____

_____

_____

_____

_____

_____

_____

_____

_____

_____

_____

_____

_____

_____

_____

_____

_____

5.RL.1, 5.RL.4, 5.RI.2, 5.RF.3, 5.RF.4, 5.W.2, 5.W.5, 5.L.4, 5.L.6, 5.OA.A.2, 5.NBT.A.4, 5.NBT.B.7

CD-104822 • © Carson-Dellosa

Day 1

1. Jordan drew a shape. The shape had 3 unequal angles. What shape could Jordan have drawn? _____

2. $246 \times 10 =$ _____

3. $12 - (\frac{1}{2} + \frac{2}{3}) =$ _____

4. $5.1 \times 10^4 =$ _____

Day 2

"I hate to put a damper on things, but Beth has a fever and will not make it tonight," explained her mom.

"Well, I never put all of my eggs in one basket," responded Ms. King. "Amanda has been our understudy for that part and knows it well. Amanda, put on Beth's costume."

1. An idiom is an expression that means something different from what it actually says. Underline any idioms in this selection. _____

2. How did Ms. King respond to the problem? _____

3. Had Amanda worked hard as the understudy? _____

4. What clues from the paragraph helped you answer question 3? _____
_____

Day 3

Write the name of the type of energy described in each sentence.

1. The food Roberto eats powers his body. _____

2. A technician X-rays a bone to see if it is broken. _____

3. Greg turns on a lamp to read. _____

4. All of the ice in a glass melts. _____

5. A power plant uses uranium to split atoms, which supply electric energy.
_____

6. Keisha takes her dog for a walk. _____

Day 4

As people spread out across America, many changes took place. The land today does not look like it did years ago. Giant trees have been cut down and the **vast** grasslands of the Midwest have become farmland for grazing cattle and raising crops. Some animals and plants have become endangered, but other species are still common.

1. Write a synonym for **vast**. _____

2. Why do you think changes to the land took place? _____
_____
_____

Name_____

To "jump the gun" means to do something earlier than expected. To "pay the piper" means you must face the consequences of your action. When someone says you are "barking up the wrong tree," they mean that you are thinking incorrectly. These phrases are idioms. Idioms are phrases that are not meant literally. To "bark up the wrong tree" does not mean that anyone is barking at a tree! Idioms are fun and interesting. Find at least four idioms on the Internet or in books, or pull them from memory. Write about what they mean. Give your report a general title. Organize your report by using subtitles, one for each separate idiom. Add illustrations if appropriate.

_____
_____
_____
_____
_____
_____
_____
_____
_____
_____
_____
_____
_____
_____
_____
_____
_____
_____
_____

Name_____

Day 1

1. $\frac{3}{4} \times \frac{1}{2}$ = _____

2. Shade the area on the grid that shows $\frac{7}{8} \times \frac{3}{4}$.

3. 236 ÷ 4 = _____

4. Write **<**, **>**, or **=** to make the statement true.

   0.59 ◯ 5.09

Day 2

I'm a very **forgetful** person, so it didn't surprise any of my friends when I shouted, "I've lost my science report!"

1. Which part of **forgetful** is the root, and which part is the suffix? _____

2. What does **forgetful** mean? _____

3. If you were reading this story aloud, describe how you would read, "I've lost my science report!" _____

4. Which point of view is this written from?
   A. first person   B. second person   C. third person

Day 3

1. Write the numbers **1** to **5** to show the order of how electricity is produced.

   A. _____ The generator makes electricity.

   B. _____ The turbine turns the drive shaft.

   C. _____ Coal burns to power the turbine.

   D. _____ Power lines deliver the electricity to the buildings.

   E. _____ The drive shaft powers the electromagnet in the generator.

Day 4

For many years, America has been called a **melting pot**. It was called that because people immigrated to America from all over the world. Most **immigrants** come to America to find a better life. Some flee their old countries because of religious or political persecution. Some bring their families, and others bring their favorite belongings. All immigrants bring their own culture.

1. What does **immigrant** mean? _____

2. Why is the phrase **melting pot** used to describe America? _____

   _____

   _____

Name_____

Imagine there is a huge snowstorm where you live. You wake up in the morning to total silence. During the night, the electricity has gone out! What would your day be like without electricity? How would it be different? What would you have to do without? What other things would you do instead? Write an essay about a day in your life without electricity. Include details to describe thoughts, feelings, or actions. Then, type it on a computer.

_____

_____

_____

_____

_____

_____

_____

_____

_____

_____

_____

_____

_____

_____

_____

_____

_____

_____

_____

_____

_____

_____

5.RL.6, 5.RI.4, 5.RF.4, 5.W.3, 5.W.5, 5.L.3, 5.L.4, 5.L.5, 5.NBT.A.3, 5.NBT.B.6, 5.NF.B.4

1. Mr. Stanford wrote 65 pages of a travel brochure. He wants to divide it into 8 equal sections. How many pages will be in each section? Write the answer as a mixed number. _____

2. Write an expression for the calculation **16 added to 10 and then divided by 2**.

   _____

3. 192 ÷ 8 = _____

4. Write four hundred thirty-six thousandths in standard form. _____

Day 1

Australia's animals are unique. They include marsupials and monotremes. Both are mammals. Marsupials carry their babies in pouches. Monotremes give birth to their young by laying eggs. However, they produce milk to feed their babies.

1. What is the subject of this passage? _____

2. Is the passage fiction or nonfiction? _____

3. What makes monotremes unique? _____

4. What makes marsupials unique? _____

5. Circle where you found your answer to number 3. Underline where you found your answer to number 4.

Day 2

Draw a line to match each word with its definition.

1. wavelength   A.   the highest point of a wave

2. crest   B.   half the distance of a wavelength

3. trough   C.   the lowest point of a wave

4. frequency   D.   the number of waves that move past a point in one second

5. amplitude   E.   the distance from one point on a wave to the same point on the next wave

Day 3

The Revolutionary War began when some colonies decided they did not want to live under British law any longer. A number of things happened to make the colonists angry with King George III. This led to a war between the people who were **loyal** to King George III (Loyalists) and others who wanted to form their own government in the new land (Patriots).

1. What does **loyal** mean? _____

   _____

2. Who was king of Britain when the Revolutionary War began? _____

3. Who were the two groups who sided against each other in this war?

   _____

Day 4

The Revolutionary War was fought between the American colonists and the British. But, not all colonists wanted independence from England. The Loyalists supported the king. They fought against the Patriots, who were sometimes neighbors and family. Imagine how people felt on both sides. Write a dialogue between two neighbors, one a Patriot and the other a Loyalist, just before the war broke out. Then, make a copy and ask another student to read the lines of one speaker while you read the lines of the other. Make changes if needed.

_____

_____

_____

_____

_____

_____

_____

_____

_____

_____

_____

_____

_____

_____

_____

_____

_____

_____

_____

_____

_____

_____

5.RI.1, 5.RI.4, 5.RI.8, 5.RF.4, 5.W.3, 5.W.4, 5.W.5, 5.L.4, 5.OA.A.2, 5.NBT.A.3, 5.NBT.B.6, 5.NF.B.3

Day 1

1. Complete the table.

2. Complete the graph based on the table.

	Add 2	Add 5
10	12	15
11		
12		
13		
14		
15		

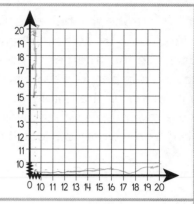

Day 2

This story continues through Week 16.
The Sydney Opera House is world famous. It is one of the most unusually designed buildings in the world. The opera house is Sydney's most famous landmark. It is located in Sydney Harbor.

1. What title would you give this passage? _____

2. Does the first paragraph tell you where Sydney is? _____

3. Do you think the opera house is near water? _____

4. What details from the paragraph helped you answer question 3? _____
   _____

Day 3

Circle the words in parentheses that correctly complete the sentences.

1. An apple looks red because the wavelength is (absorbed, reflected).

2. A white shirt looks white because the beam of light is (refracted, scattered).

3. Only the blue wavelength will be (absorbed, transmitted) when a blue filter covers a flashlight.

4. You can see smoke because part of the light is (transmitted, scattered) by the smoke particles, while the other part is (transmitted, scattered) through the light.

5. A curtain that is (opaque, translucent) will keep all light from entering a room.

Day 4

Various events caused the colonists' disloyalty to their king. In 1763, the king **forbade** western expansion. In 1765, the colonists were forced to give food and shelter to British soldiers. Then, the king forced colonists to pay a tax on all kinds of paper and other goods. In 1770, colonists were killed and **injured** in the Boston Massacre. In 1773, the king placed a tax on tea. These events led to the Declaration of Independence in 1776.

1. What is the main idea of this paragraph? _____
   _____

2. Write a synonym for **injured**. _____

3. Write an antonym for **forbade**. _____

Think about the number zero. Do you think of it as nothing? At first thought, it does not seem like much. Yet some mathematicians have said that it is the most important of all numbers. Use the Internet or books to find out about the history of zero. Early peoples did not have a number for zero. Find out why some people think zero is such a special number. Write a report on the history of zero, including when it was first used. Then, do some thinking. What would it be like if there was no zero today? Organize your report in paragraphs. In the last paragraph, write your opinion about this interesting number.

_____

_____

_____

_____

_____

_____

_____

_____

_____

_____

_____

_____

_____

_____

_____

_____

_____

_____

_____

_____

_____

_____

1. $94 \times 0.67 =$ _____

2. Mark ran 875 miles this year in the track club. Mark ran in 52 track meets and ran the same number of miles in each. How many miles did Mark run in each track meet? Write the answer as a mixed number. _____

3. Write an expression for the calculation **4 times the difference of 10 and 8 minus 3.**

   _____

4. Write **<**, **>**, or **=** to make the statement true.   3.03 ◯ 3.3

This story began on Week 13.

Danish architect Jørn Utzon designed the Sydney Opera House. He won a contest for his design. Work began in 1959 and was completed in 1973. The estimate for the Sydney Opera House was $7 million (Australian). However, the final cost was $102 million.

1. Does this paragraph give you a clue about where Sydney is? If so, where?

   _____

2. How long did it take to build the Sydney Opera House? _____

3. How much was the building estimated to cost? _____

4. Was the cost estimate accurate? Explain. _____

Write **true** or **false**. Rewrite any false statements to make them true.

1. _____ Every cell has a nucleus.

2. _____ Cells are the basic units of matter.

3. _____ A cell will divide and make two cells that are exactly the same.

4. _____ Organs are made of similar cells that work together.

5. _____ Chromosomes in one cell are the same as in the other new cell.

The **Declaration of Independence** was written to explain why the colonies had chosen to separate from England. The Revolutionary War had already begun and the colonies had cut many of their ties to England. Thomas Jefferson was chosen to draft the letter. He had the help of a committee that included Benjamin Franklin and John Adams. The document is dated July 4, 1776.

1. What was the purpose of the **Declaration of Independence**? _____

   _____

2. What American holiday is linked to this event? _____

3. Name three Americans involved in writing this document. _____

   _____

Name_____

   Imagine that the mayor of your town or city has announced that there are millions of dollars left over in the budget. He would like to build something for the community to enjoy. Write a letter to the mayor to tell him what you would like to see built. Give reasons to support your opinion. Then, type it on a computer. Be sure that your letter is respectful in tone. Show it to your teacher. Make changes if needed. Consider sending it to your own mayor.

_____

_____

_____

_____

_____

_____

_____

_____

_____

_____

_____

_____

_____

_____

_____

_____

_____

_____

_____

_____

_____

_____

5.RI.1, 5.RI.3, 5.RI.8, 5.RI.10, 5.W.1, 5.W.4, 5.W.6, 5.OA.A.2, 5.NBT.A.3, 5.NBT.B.7, 5.NF.B.3   CD-104822 • © Carson-Dellosa

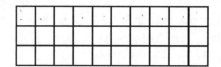

1. $\frac{2}{3} \times 8 =$ _____

2. Shade the area on the grid that shows $\frac{2}{3} \times \frac{3}{10}$.

3. $1,870 \div 34 =$ _____

4. $1.9 \times 10^3 =$ _____

Day 1

This story began on Week 13.

Utzon wanted the roof to look like sails on a giant sailing ship. Some people think the roof looks like huge seashells. The roof is made of 10 gigantic arched-concrete shell shapes. The shells have ribs that curve inward. Concrete joins the ribs where they meet. One of the biggest cranes in the world lifted the concrete roof pieces into place. Working on the building was dangerous because of the roof.

1. Does the Sydney Opera House look like Utzon wanted it to? _____

2. What clues helped you answer question 1? _____

3. What holds the ribs of the shells in place? _____

4. What do you think the danger was with the roof? _____

Day 2

Write words from the word bank to complete the passage.

| characteristics | kingdoms | organisms | species |

Scientists refer to all living things in the world as _____. An organism can be grouped into one of six main groups. These six groups, called _____, include plants, animals, protists, eubacteria, archaebacteria, and fungi. These are the largest groups in which organisms can be placed for identification. After kingdoms, organisms can be further divided by various _____ that they share. _____ is the smallest and most specific group into which organisms can be divided.

Day 3

The Revolutionary War began in 1775. The Battles of Lexington and Concord began the war on April 19, 1775. A gunshot went off during a face-off between the British and about 80 militiamen. Ralph Waldo Emerson called this gunshot "the shot heard round the world" in a poem. The war lasted until 1783.

1. How many years did the Revolutionary War last? _____

2. Why do you think Emerson called the first shot "the shot heard round the world"?

_____

_____

Day 4

There are six kingdoms of living things: plants, animals, protists, eubacteria, archaebacteria, and fungi. Choose an organism from one of these kingdoms. Research the organism, then write a report about it. Define and explain facts or details about how it eats, reproduces, moves, etc. Include a list of your sources at the bottom of your report. Show your report to your teacher. Revise if needed.

_____

_____

_____

_____

_____

_____

_____

_____

_____

_____

_____

_____

_____

_____

_____

_____

_____

_____

_____

_____

_____

_____

5.RI.1, 5.RI.4, 5.RI.8, 5.RI.10, 5.W.2, 5.W.7, 5.W.8, 5.W.10, 5.L.5, 5.L.6, 5.NBT.A.2, 5.NBT.B.6, 5.NF.B.4

1. 0.81 ÷ 0.9 = _____

2. 10 thousands = _____ ones

$\frac{2}{3}$ in.

3. Find the area of the rectangle.   3 in.

_____

4. 135 × 85 = _____

This story began on Week 13.
The opera house contains one hall for operas. The orchestra plays in another hall. A third hall is for plays. A fourth is for chamber music. The fifth is for exhibitions.

1. What fraction of halls are used for music? _____

2. What kind of music do orchestras and chamber music groups play?

   A. hip-hop   B. classical   C. contemporary country

3. Which, if any, of the activities that take place in the Sydney Opera House would you enjoy? Explain. _____

4. What kind of music or other event do you think they should have at the opera house? _____

Use each word in a sentence to tell why it is important to plants.

1. photosynthesis _____

_____

2. chlorophyll _____

_____

3. carbon dioxide _____

_____

In 1803, the United States only had 17 states. President Thomas Jefferson wanted to expand the country. He chose Meriwether Lewis to explore the West. Jefferson wanted Lewis to make maps of the new lands. He wanted him to find a river big enough so ships could sail to the ocean. Finally, Lewis was to make friends with the American Indians he met. Lewis and his friend, William Clark, did all three. It took a year and a half.

1. How many states were part of the United States in 1803? _____

2. Why do you think Jefferson wanted Lewis and Clark to befriend American Indians?

_____

3. Would you volunteer for a trip like this? Explain. _____

_____

On Lewis and Clark's expedition, they met some new animals. One of the animals they discovered as they crossed the plains was the prairie dog. Imagine that you are an explorer. You have just found an animal you have never seen or heard of. Write about this animal. Describe its size and appearance, its habitat, and daily habits. Include how it gets its food. Type your report on a computer. Add illustrations.

_____

_____

_____

_____

_____

_____

_____

_____

_____

_____

_____

_____

_____

_____

_____

_____

_____

_____

_____

5.RI.1, 5.RI.10, 5.W.3, 5.W.6, 5.NBT.A.1, 5.NBT.B.5, 5.NBT.B.7, 5.NF.B.4

CD-104822 • © Carson-Dellosa

Day 1

1. Write 4.510 in word form. _____

2. Round 51.65 to the nearest whole number. _____

3. $\frac{3}{4} \times 5 =$ _____

4. $(2 \times 7) - (2 \times 5) =$ _____

Day 2

Television does not have just one inventor. In the late 1800s, an Italian inventor named Guglielmo Marconi set the stage when he discovered how to send signals through the air as electromagnetic waves. His invention was the radio. In the early 1900s, a young American named Philo Farnsworth had an idea to send pictures as well as sound through the air. This led to the invention of the electronic television camera.

1. What other invention set the stage for the invention of the television? _____

2. Whose invention led to the electronic television camera? _____

3. About how many years have passed between that invention and now? _____

4. What is the main idea of this paragraph? _____

Day 3

1. Unscramble the letters in parentheses to complete the sentences. Then, write the letters **A** to **E** to show the correct order. _____, _____, _____, _____, _____

   A. The bee _____ (lanstoplie) the pistil of another plant.

   B. Sperm cells in pollen grow on the _____(matnes). Egg cells are found in the ovules deep inside the _____ (iplist).

   C. A tube grows down from the pollen, through the pistil, and into an _____ (lovue).

   D. A sperm cell _____ (terzilfies) an egg cell.

   E. _____ (nelplo) sticks to a bee as it gathers nectar.

Day 4

Sacagawea was 12 when she was **taken captive** and moved far east of her tribe's homelands in the early 1800s. Meriwether Lewis and William Clark met her near the beginning of their expedition. They asked her and her husband to guide them. Sacagawea helped Lewis and Clark in many ways. She worked as an **interpreter** when they met different tribes. Her memory of landmarks helped to guide them west.

1. Write a word that means the same as **taken captive**. _____

2. What is an **interpreter**? _____

3. What is the main idea of the story? _____

_____

Imagine you are the new teacher in a second-grade class. There will be 20 seven-year-olds in your math class. How will you teach math to these children? What will you do to make the class interesting? How will you help students who have difficulties? Try to remember back to when you were in second grade. Write an essay describing the kind of math teacher you would be. Include details to describe thoughts, feelings, or actions.

_____

_____

_____

_____

_____

_____

_____

_____

_____

_____

_____

_____

_____

_____

_____

_____

_____

_____

_____

_____

_____

_____

_____

5.RI.1, 5.RI.2, 5.RI.3, 5.RI.4, 5.RI.10, 5.RF.4, 5.W.3, 5.W.8, 5.L.5, 5.L.6, 5.OA.A.1, 5.NBT.A.3, 5.NBT.A.4, 5.NF.B.4

Day 1

1. 803 × 31 = _____

2. Holly is making a stir-fry. Holly measures $\frac{5}{8}$ cup of chicken and then adds $\frac{1}{9}$ cup more. How much chicken does Holly use altogether? _____

3. What is the value of 6 in 3.567? _____

4. Write **<**, **>**, or **=** to make the statement true.

   24.856 ◯ 24.865

Day 2

Circle the choice that shows the correct capitalization.
1. A. tuesday, january 22   B. tuesday, January 22   C. Tuesday, January 22

Circle the correct word.
2. (He, Him) and Brooke are (hour, our) cousins.

Mark the sentence to add the missing punctuation.
3. Kate and Luis entered the capsule

Circle the correct word for the sentence.
4. My dad (lies, lays) in the hammock for hours.

Day 3

1. Unscramble the letters in parentheses to complete the paragraph.

   All plants and animals adapt to better survive in their environment. Any adaptations that relate to the body of an animal or a plant are _____ (sutarcrlut) adaptations. Adaptations that affect how an animal or a plant reacts to situations are _____ (hovibealra) adaptations. _____ (malgeofacu) is a structural adaptation that helps animals and plants blend into their surroundings. Some animals and plants use a behavioral adaptation called _____ (irmcymi) to fool predators into thinking they are another species.

Day 4

The pre-Columbian era refers to the history of the Americas before Columbus arrived. It also names the history and culture of the American Indian groups in the United States at that time. They were the cliff dwellers and pueblo people of the Southwest, the tribes of the Pacific Northwest, the **nomadic** nations of the Great Plains, and the woodland tribes east of the Mississippi River.

1. What does **nomadic** mean? _____

2. In the pre-Columbian era, who lived in what we now call the United States?

   _____

   _____

All plants and animals adapt to survive in their environment. Choose an animal that uses camouflage to survive in its environment. Use books, magazines, or the Internet to research this animal. How do its habits, colorings, markings, etc., allow for its survival? Where is this animal's habitat? Who are its predators? What animals does it prey on? Use facts, details, and definitions to explain or inform. When you are finished writing, show your report to a classmate. Ask her to edit your report for correct capitalization, spelling, and grammar. Revise if needed.

_____

_____

_____

_____

_____

_____

_____

_____

_____

_____

_____

_____

_____

_____

_____

_____

_____

_____

_____

_____

_____

_____

_____

5.RI.1, 5.RI.4, 5.RI.7, 5.RI.10, 5.W.2, 5.W.5, 5.W.10, 5.L.1, 5.L.2, 5.L.6, 5.NBT.A.1, 5.NBT.A.3, 5.NBT.B.5, 5.NF.A.2

CD-104822 • © Carson-Dellosa

Name_____

1. Complete the table.

2. Complete the graph based on the table.

	Add 1	Add 2
30	31	32
31		
32		
33		
34		
35		

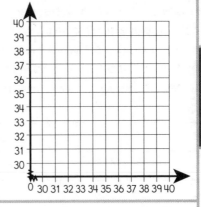

Hair protects the body. It acts as a cushion, protecting the head from bumps and bruises. Hair can be a shield from the hot summer sun and keep the head warm on chilly winter days. Inside the nose and ears, tiny hairs **deter** dirt, dust, and insects from entering the body. Eyebrows are patches of hair that trap **perspiration** before it is able to reach the eyes. Eyelashes prevent dirt and dust from infecting the eyes.

1. Which syllable do you emphasize when you say **deter**? _____

2. List the word that means **deter**. _____

3. What is another word for **perspiration**? _____

4. What hair protects our eyes? _____

Write **I** for each inherited trait. Write **L** for each learned behavior.

1. _____ riding a bike

2. _____ size 8 feet

3. _____ chewing with your mouth closed

4. _____ playing baseball

5. _____ blue eyes

6. _____ curly hair

7. _____ enjoying comedy movies

8. _____ attached earlobes

Climate and geography determined much in early American Indian life. The Southwestern hunter-gatherer nations lived in cliff **dwellings** or rock-and-plaster homes. The Northwestern nations ate fish, often salmon, and lived in wooden shelters. The Plains tribes lived in tepees and hunted game, primarily buffalo. The woodland tribes hunted forest animals, grew vegetables, and lived in wooden huts.

1. Write a synonym for **dwelling**. _____

2. Choose one of the nations above. Explain how climate and geography determined its choices. _____

_____

You are a mixture of inherited traits and learned behaviors. Write an essay to describe yourself in these terms. Start with a description of yourself. How many of the characteristics you name would also describe someone in your family? How many are behaviors you learned on your own? Use subtitles to divide the rest of the essay into *Inherited Traits* and *Learned Behaviors*. Show your essay to someone in your family. Make changes if necessary.

_____

_____

_____

_____

_____

_____

_____

_____

_____

_____

_____

_____

_____

_____

_____

_____

_____

_____

_____

_____

_____

_____

_____

_____

_____

_____

_____

 5.RI.1, 5.RI.4, 5.RI.10, 5.RF.3, 5.RF.4, 5.W.3, 5.W.4, 5.W.5, 5.W.10, 5.L.5, 5.OA.B.3 — CD-104822 • © Carson-Dellosa

Name_____

Day 1

1. 47 × 0.76 = _____

2. Write 437.04 in expanded form. _____

3. Ms. Benson has 89 yards of string. If she wants to give each of her 15 students an equal amount of string, how much will each student get? Write the answer as a mixed number. _____

4. 0.1 ÷ 0.2 = _____

Day 2

Circle the choice that shows the correct capitalization.
1. A. Our teacher is mr. Conti.   B. Our teacher is Mr. Conti.

Circle the correct word.
2. (Affects/Effects) of the earthquake are everywhere (accept, except) the shelter.

Add the missing punctuation to the sentence.
3. What is their mission

Circle the correct word for the sentence.
4. Michael has (lain, laid) his scissors on the desk.

Day 3

Write **true** or **false**. Rewrite any false statements to make them true.

1. _____ Ecosystems always stay the same.

2. _____ Animals can easily adapt to living in different ecosystems.

3. _____ Ecosystems must include nonliving things such as soil, air, and water.

4. _____ Humans are part of ecosystems.

5. _____ If one type of animal in an ecosystem goes extinct, nothing happens.

Day 4

Life on a plantation was difficult. Slaves worked in the big house of a plantation. They cooked, sewed, and cleaned. Slave women often took care of the owner's children and had little time to take care of their own. Some slaves worked in the fields to plant and harvest crops. They fixed fences and fed farm animals. They worked long hours in the blazing sun. All slaves lived in the shadow of the master of a plantation. Some owners treated their slaves cruelly.

1. What were some of the jobs that slaves did? _____
_____
_____

2. What do you think was the hardest part of being a slave? Explain. _____
_____

Think about what you know about the daily lives of slaves and how they were treated. The institution of slavery was unjust. Unfortunately, most slaves could not escape this injustice. Think about a time when you had to deal with an unfair or unjust situation in your life. What was it? How did you feel? How did you handle it? In the end, were you able to make the situation just and fair or is it still ongoing? Write a narrative that tells about this time. Include details to describe thoughts, feelings, and actions. Include dialogue in your narrative. Provide a conclusion.

_____

_____

_____

_____

_____

_____

_____

_____

_____

_____

_____

_____

_____

_____

_____

_____

_____

_____

_____

_____

_____

_____

5.RI.1, 5.RI.10, 5.W.3, 5.W.8, 5.L.1, 5.L.2, 5.NBT.A.3, 5.NBT.B.7, 5.NF.B.3

1. Leslie needs 48 ounces of charcoal for her grill. How many pounds of charcoal should she buy? _____

2. (72 ÷ 9) × 5 = _____

Boxes of O-Shaped Cereal in Pounds

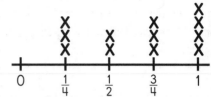

3. Nadia bought boxes of o-shaped cereal at the grocery store. The line plot below shows the different amounts of boxed cereal Nadia bought. How many pounds of o-shaped cereal did Nadia buy altogether? _____

The 1850 census showed that about 4 million African Americans were living in the United States. Only 400,000 of these African Americans were free. Free African Americans had to obey laws established for them. They were not allowed to socialize with slaves. They also could not hold meetings.

1. What is the main idea of this paragraph? _____

2. What word has the **s** sound at the beginning, middle, and end? _____

3. Why were free African Americans not able to socialize with slaves? _____

_____

4. Why did the author include this paragraph in a biography about the slave Clara Brown? _____

1. Complete the illustration with four other animals to show how energy moves in a food chain.

2. Label the organisms in your food chain using **consumer**, **energy**, and **producer**.

3. What kind of discussion would this illustration support? _____

_____

On January 1, 1863, President Abraham Lincoln issued an executive order that freed the slaves living in Confederate states. This was called the **Emancipation** Proclamation. The original copy is in the National Archives in Washington, D.C. It is five pages long and was originally tied with thin red and blue ribbons. The last page holds President Lincoln's signature.

1. What does **emancipation** mean? _____

2. How did this document impact the Confederate states after the Civil War?

_____

Name_____

Imagine that a cereal truck swerved in front of your house. It dumped 50 cartons of cereal on your lawn and kept on going. Your family was unable to find the owner of this cereal, so you can't return it. What will you do with all this cereal? Consider these cereal facts before writing your essay. Each carton contains eight boxes of cereal. The average person eats about 160 bowls of cereal in a year. Most boxes of cereal contain seven or eight one-cup servings. Do the math—that's a lot of cereal in your living room! Find a creative solution to the problem using any or all of the cereal facts given to you.

_____

_____

_____

_____

_____

_____

_____

_____

_____

_____

_____

_____

_____

_____

_____

_____

_____

_____

_____

_____

_____

_____

_____

_____

5.RI.1, 5.RI.2, 5.RI.3, 5.RI.8, 5.RI.10, 5.RF.4, 5.W.3, 5.SL.5, 5.L.4, 5.L.6, 5.OA.A.1, 5.MD.A.1, 5.MD.B.2

1. $687 \times 0.30 =$ _____

2. Write an expression for the calculation **12 added to 56 divided by 7**.

_____

3. Find the volume of the figure by counting unit cubes.

_____ cubic units

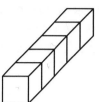

4. What is the value of 1 in the number 58.132?

_____

Lewis and Clark's exploration led to fur trading in the West. Several companies competed with each other. They sold pelts around the world. They had to hire men to get furs for them. The trappers, who trapped deer, beaver, and muskrat, became known as mountain men. People of different races worked together in the fur trade. One of those men was an African American named James Beckwourth.

1. What is a good title for this passage? _____

2. What job did James Beckwourth have? _____

3. Was the fur trade an equal opportunity employer? _____

4. What clues from the paragraph helped you answer question 3? _____

Draw a line to match each word with its definition.

1. ecosystem

2. habitat

3. population

4. environment

5. community

A. the place where an animal lives, where all of its needs can be met

B. all of the populations that live in a place

C. all of the living and nonliving things in a place

D. a group of one kind of living thing that lives in a place

E. everything that is around a living thing

The Mayflower Compact of 1620 was America's first written plan of government. The Declaration of Independence declared freedom from England in 1776. The Articles of Confederation established a central government and was ratified in 1781. The US Constitution was adopted in 1787 and provided a stronger government and more freedom for citizens. The Bill of Rights added 10 amendments to the Constitution in 1791, strengthening citizens' freedoms.

1. Which of these historical documents do you think was most important?

_____

2. Explain your answer to question 1. _____

_____

It is the year 1825. Imagine that you are a fur trader. You have ridden on horseback to a trading post with a huge bundle of animal pelts. The trader has offered you a single price for all of your pelts. But, you feel that he is trying to cheat you. What could you say to persuade him to give you a fair price for your pelts? Write a likely dialogue between you and the trader. Remember that the year is 1825. When you are finished, make a copy. Ask another student to read the lines of the fur trader as you read your own lines. Then, make changes if necessary.

_____
_____
_____
_____
_____
_____
_____
_____
_____
_____
_____
_____
_____
_____
_____
_____
_____
_____
_____
_____
_____

Day 1

1. Write 41.344 in word form. _____

2. Pablo drove 129 minutes on Monday. He drove 98 minutes on Tuesday and 73 minutes on Wednesday. How many hours did Pablo spend driving altogether?

   _____

3. $(14 \times 10 + 45) - (56 - 39) =$ _____

4. Round 3.288 to the nearest hundredth.

   _____

Day 2

Circle the choice that shows the correct capitalization.
1. A. *The house on the hill*   B. *The House on the Hill*   C. *The House On the Hill*

Circle the correct word.
2. Every one of (us, we) boys passed (their, his) test.

Mark the sentence to add the missing punctuation.
3. Look out It's an asteroid

Circle the correct word for the sentence.
4. The papers have (laid, lain) on the desk for weeks.

Day 3

Unscramble the letters in parentheses to complete the sentences.

1. The phases of the moon make the _____ (runal) cycle.

2. A _____ (feil) cycle describes how an organism grows and reproduces.

3. The _____ (yoxeng) cycle explains how producers and consumers work together to make the air they need to survive.

4. Plants use the cycle of _____ (stesithhoopnys) to make sugar they need for energy.

Day 4

The US Constitution sets forth how Americans will pay for government. It is through taxation. The Sixteenth Amendment was added to the Constitution in 1913. It gives Congress the right to tax individuals according to the amount of income they earn. Taxes pay the expenses of government, which include the president's salary, some education costs, the building of some roads and bridges, and many other things.

1. List ways the government spends the money received from taxing individuals' incomes. _____

2. Do you think the Sixteenth Amendment is fair? Explain. _____

   _____

Many of nature's cycles are interrelated. For one cycle to continue, it needs the help of another. For instance, the cycle of tides is affected by the cycle of the moon. Choose two cycles. Tell how they work together. Then, explain why they are important to the balance of nature. Use the Internet or books for your research. Include a list of your sources at the bottom of your report. Type your finished report on the computer.

_____

_____

_____

_____

_____

_____

_____

_____

_____

_____

_____

_____

_____

_____

_____

_____

_____

_____

_____

_____

_____

_____

_____

_____

5.RI.10, 5.W.2, 5.W.7, 5.W.8, 5.L.1, 5.L.2, 5.L.6, 5.OA.A.1, 5.NBT.A.3, 5.NF.B.4, 5.MD.A.1

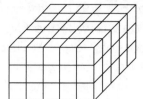

Day 1

1. Find the volume of the figure by counting unit cubes.

    _____ cubic units

2. Round 92.471 to the nearest tenth. _____

3. 304 ÷ 8 = _____

4. (31 × 15) + (108 ÷ 6) = _____

Day 2

This story continues through Week 27.
In 1838, the United States Government made the Cherokee move from their homes in Georgia and other states to what was then called the Indian Territory. That land is now the state of Oklahoma.

1. What is a good title for this passage? _____

2. Does the first paragraph tell us anything about who the Cherokee were? Explain.
    _____

3. What is the Indian Territory called today? _____

4. How long ago did the events in this passage take place? _____

Day 3

1. Unscramble the letters in parentheses to complete the paragraph about the nervous system.

    The _____ (sovernu) system helps people sense their environment. It consists of the _____ (nabir), the spinal cord, and nerves. _____ (preetrocs), like the eyes, ears, and skin, sense changes outside the body. Inside, _____ (sronag), like the heart and the stomach, sense changes in chemicals and body fluids. The data travels through the nerves and _____ (nilpas) cord to the brain. It processes the information. It sends a signal telling the body how to _____ (crate).

Day 4

Americans enjoy many rights. Their rights range from freedom of speech to freedom to practice their religion of choice. Other rights include the freedom to a trial by a jury. Many of the rights of Americans are protected by the first 10 amendments to the US Constitution, or the Bill of Rights. The Bill of Rights was ratified in 1791 and has stood for more than 200 years.

1. Write two words from the passage that are synonyms. _____

2. What might happen without freedom of speech? _____
    _____

Imagine that you are the president of your class. You decide that your class needs a bill of rights. You will write the Class Bill of Rights, but you, two classmates, and your teacher must sign it. If possible, talk to several other students before beginning your writing. It is important that the rights of all of your classmates are considered. Then, write a Class Bill of Rights. It should take up at least one full page and include 10 or more rights. Give reasons to support your opinions. Type it on a computer. Show it to your teacher and the students you have chosen to sign it. Make changes if needed.

_____
_____
_____
_____
_____
_____
_____
_____
_____
_____
_____
_____
_____
_____
_____
_____
_____
_____
_____
_____
_____

5.RI.1, 5.RI.4, 5.RI.10, 5.W.1, 5.W.4, 5.W.6, 5.L.5, 5.L.6, 5.OA.A.1, 5.NBT.A.4, 5.NBT.B.6, 5.MD.C.4

Day 1

1. Write 0.955 in expanded form. _____

2. $21 \div \frac{1}{3} =$ _____

3. Mr. Freeman asked his students what fraction of an hour they spend talking on their cell phones each night. Use the data shown to create a line plot.

$\frac{1}{2}, \frac{1}{4}, \frac{1}{2}, \frac{1}{4}, \frac{3}{4}, \frac{1}{4}, \frac{1}{2}, \frac{3}{4}$

Day 2

This story began on Week 24.
The Cherokee had to walk for hundreds of miles, and they often did not have enough food or water. Many hundreds of them died. The mothers felt so sad that some of them could not take care of their children.

1. How did the Cherokee get to Indian Territory? _____

2. Does the author include any opinions in this paragraph? _____

3. Who is feeling sad in this paragraph? _____

4. This journey is called the Trail of Tears. Underline the clues that tell why.

Day 3

1. Why is it important to eat a healthful diet? Give two reasons.

_____
_____
_____

2. Why should you eat foods of all different colors?

_____
_____

Day 4

The founding fathers, who wrote the US Constitution, did not want one person or group of people to have too much control. The powers of the national government are **distributed** among the legislative, executive, and judicial branches. Each one has separate responsibilities and obligations, but they must work together to keep the country running smoothly.

1. Write a synonym for **distributed**. _____

2. Name the three branches of government. _____
_____

3. Why was it important to separate the government into separate branches?
_____

Many schools have strict rules about allowing students to have cell phones in school. This is a problem for students and teachers. There are definite benefits to allowing cell phones in schools. But, there are also drawbacks. What do you think? Do you think cell phones should be allowed in school? Write a letter to your principal to explain your position on this issue. Give reasons to support your opinion. If this is an actual issue in your school, share your essay with your principal.

_____

_____

_____

_____

_____

_____

_____

_____

_____

_____

_____

_____

_____

_____

_____

_____

_____

_____

_____

_____

_____

_____

_____

_____

1. $215 \times 0.71 =$ _____

2.   Find the area of the rectangle.

     _____

$\frac{2}{3}$ in.

8 in.

3. $\frac{3}{16} + \frac{1}{6} =$ _____

2 ft.

4.   Find the volume of the cube. _____ cubic feet

This story began on Week 24.
According to the legend, the chiefs asked the Great One for a sign that would make the mothers feel better and make them strong enough to take care of their children.

1.   Who in the tribe created a solution to the problem? _____

2.   What solution did the tribe create for the mothers? _____

3.   Who do you think the Great One was? _____

4.   If you were the Great One, what kind of sign would you send to make the mothers feel better and be stronger? _____

     _____

Write words from the word bank to complete the sentences. Not all words will be used.

| atmosphere | exosphere | gravity | mesosphere |
| stratosphere | thermosphere | troposphere | |

1.   The _____ is about 500 miles (805 km) high.

2.   It is held close to Earth because of _____.

3.   We live in the _____.

4.   The top layer, which is space, is the _____.

5.   Ozone gas is in the _____ layer.

The powers of the legislative branch of government include the power to **impeach** the president. They can also **nominate** members of the federal judiciary. They have the power to pass laws over the president's veto by two-thirds majority vote of both houses of Congress, and to establish committees to oversee activities of the executive branch. Congress is composed of two parts, the Senate and the House of Representatives.

1.   What does **impeach** mean? _____

2.   Write a synonym for **nominate**. _____

3.   What are the two parts of Congress? _____

In 1829, settlers found gold on the land where the ancient Cherokee lived. The settlers went to the US government and asked them to force the Cherokee to leave the land so they could get the rights to it. In all, almost 17,000 Cherokee were forced to move to what is now Oklahoma. Their long walk was called the Trail of Tears. What do you think about this historical event? Do you think something like this could happen today? Why or why not? Use the Internet or books to find any facts you need. Use facts and definitions to explain or inform. Give reasons to support your opinion.

_____

_____

_____

_____

_____

_____

_____

_____

_____

_____

_____

_____

_____

_____

_____

_____

_____

_____

_____

_____

_____

_____

_____

5.RI.1, 5.RI.3, 5.RI.10, 5.RF.4, 5.W.1, 5.W.2, 5.W.8, 5.L.5, 5.L.6, 5.NBT.B.7, 5.NF.A.1, 5.NF.B.4, 5.MD.C.5

1. $\frac{4}{15} + \frac{3}{5} =$ _____

2. _____ thousands = 1,800 tens

3. $(3.4 + 6.6) \times (1.8 + 2.7) =$ _____

8 ft.

4. Find the volume of the cube. _____ cubic inches

This story began on Week 24.

The Great One promised that where a mother's tear fell, a flower would grow. It is called the Cherokee rose. It is white, which stands for the mothers' tears. The flower's center is gold, a symbol of the gold that was taken from the tribe's land. The seven leaves on the stem stand for the seven groups who walked along the Trail of Tears.

1. What is the Cherokee rose? _____

2. How did the legend of the Cherokee rose come about? _____

3. What are the different parts of the rose, and what are they symbols of? _____
   _____

4. How does this story make you feel? _____

Write **true** or **false**. Rewrite any false statements to make them true.

1. _____ Most of Earth's water is in the oceans.

2. _____ Animals play a part in the water cycle through transpiration.

3. _____ Without the sun, the water cycle would not exist.

4. _____ Freshwater is contained in rivers, lakes, and glaciers.

5. _____ The water cycle does not affect the weather.

The main job of the executive branch of the US government is to run the government and its independent agencies. The executive branch is **composed** of the president, vice president, and cabinet members. The executive branch carries out federal laws and recommends new ones

1. What is the main job of the executive branch? _____
   _____

2. Write a synonym for **composed**. _____

3. Who makes up the executive branch? _____
   _____

Write a public service announcement to explain the importance of freshwater. Use the Internet or books to find more information. Present the basic facts. Then, offer three ways that people can preserve freshwater's cleanliness. Type your information on a computer and add illustrations. Consider a brochure format.

_____

_____

_____

_____

_____

_____

_____

_____

_____

_____

_____

_____

_____

_____

_____

_____

_____

_____

_____

_____

_____

_____

_____

5.RI.1, 5.RI.10, 5.RF.4, 5.W.2, 5.W.4, 5.W.8, 5.L.5, 5.OA.A.1, 5.NBT.A.1, 5.NF.A.1, 5.MD.C.5

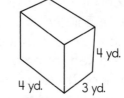

Day 1

1. Round 67.62 to the nearest whole number.

   _____

2. Find the volume of the cube. _____ cubic yards

   4 yd.
   4 yd.   3 yd.

3. Write **<**, **>**, or **=** to make the statement true.   6.42 ◯ 64.2

4. Write an expression for the calculation **double the number 15 and then add 25 divided by 5**.

Day 2

Use proofreading marks to correct the capitalization errors.
   1. did the movie *around the world in 80 days* win an academy award in 1956?

Draw a line under the complete predicate. Circle the predicate verb.
   2. Jayla and I cheered for our favorite team.

Add quotation marks, capitalization, underlines, and punctuation where necessary.
   3. The Olympic Games were held in Stockholm Sweden in 1912 replied valerie

Circle the correct words in the sentence.
   4. My library book was (dew/due) last (week/weak).

Day 3

1. What is the difference between weather and climate? Explain. Then, discuss with a partner.

   _____
   _____
   _____
   _____

Day 4

The judicial branch of the US government studies the laws and makes decisions about what laws mean and how laws should be followed in different situations. The judicial branch can also **propose** amendments to the US Constitution. It is made up of the court system, which includes the Supreme Court and lower federal courts.

   1. What is the job of the judicial branch? _____

   _____

   2. Write a synonym for **propose**. _____

   3. Name the two parts of the court system. _____

   _____

The Supreme Court is often called "the highest court in the land." Its decisions are absolute and final. Imagine that you are a Supreme Court Justice. You are asked to settle an argument. The case is about two teenagers who wore black armbands to school to protest the war. They were asked to remove the armbands. When they refused, the students were suspended from school. The parents of the students have sued the school saying their rights to free speech have been violated. Write an essay expressing your opinion on this matter. Give reasons to support your opinions.

_____

_____

_____

_____

_____

_____

_____

_____

_____

_____

_____

_____

_____

_____

_____

_____

_____

_____

_____

_____

_____

_____

5.RI.1, 5.RF.4, 5.W.1, 5.W.3, 5.W.4, 5.SL.1, 5.L.1, 5.L.2, 5.L.5, 5.OA.A.2, 5.NBT.A.3, 5.NBT.A.4, 5.MD.C.5 CD-104822 • © Carson-Dellosa

1. 285 ÷ 5 = _____

2. Chase conducts a survey of his friends to find out what fraction of their money is spent on clothes. Use the data shown to create a line plot.

$$\frac{1}{8}, \frac{5}{8}, \frac{3}{4}, \frac{7}{8}, \frac{1}{4}, \frac{1}{4}, \frac{1}{8}, \frac{5}{8}, \frac{1}{8}, \frac{3}{4}$$

George Washington Carver wanted to go to a college. The college refused to admit him because he was African American. But, George refused to give up. Finally, he went to college. He was an excellent student. He took botany and chemistry classes.

1. Does George give up easily? _____

2. What clues helped you answer question 1? _____

3. What kind of classes are botany and chemistry: **literature** or **science**? _____

4. What clues tell you whether George was a hard worker? _____

_____

1. How does the shape of Earth affect climate?

_____

_____

_____

2. How does the tilt of Earth affect climate?

_____

_____

_____

The president heads the executive branch of the United States. The length of a president's term is four years, although the president may be elected for a second term. Presidential candidates must have been born a citizen of the United States, be at least 35 years old, and have been a resident of the United States for at least 14 years.

1. Name the current US president. _____

2. Would you like to be president of the United States? Explain. _____

_____

_____

Name_____

What do you spend the largest amount of time on? Is it video games, homework, sports or the Internet? Why? Do you feel that you spend your free time wisely? Would your family agree? Make a line plot of your free time on another sheet of paper. Divide it by the various activities and hours that you spend on those activities throughout the week. Then, write an essay to justify how you spend your free time. Give reasons to support your opinions. Allow another student to read your essay. Make changes if needed.

_____
_____
_____
_____
_____
_____
_____
_____
_____
_____
_____
_____
_____
_____
_____
_____
_____
_____
_____
_____
_____
_____
_____
_____

Day 1

1. $\frac{6}{7} - \frac{5}{9} =$ _____

2. $648 \times 0.85 =$ _____

3. Norman is shipping 2 boxes. The first box weighs 4,180 grams, and the second box weighs 820 grams. If shipping costs $6.43 per kilogram, how much does Norman spend on shipping? _____

4. 4 tenths = _____ hundredths

Day 2

Use proofreading marks to correct the capitalization errors.
1. robert burns, the poet, wrote "auld lang syne."

Draw a line under the complete predicate. Circle the predicate verb.
2. Chris dropped one more quarter into the machine.

Add quotation marks, capitalization, underlines, and punctuation where necessary.
3. Monica yelled Wow did you see that car

Circle the correct words in the sentence.
4. Did those (ate/eight) (flowers/flours) come from your yard?

Day 3

1. (Weathering, Deposition) is the settling of rocks and soil once it has been eroded.

2. The materials fall out once the water or wind (quickens, slows).

3. The soil in these areas is filled with rich (nutrients, gases) that are good for crops.

4. Depositions caused by wind can form (mountains, dunes).

5. Depositions caused by ocean water can form new (bays, beaches).

6. In a river, deposition can create a (delta, canyon).

Day 4

The American system of government is based on the **concept** of democracy. The word **democracy** comes from the Greek word *demokratia*, which means "people rule." In a democracy, people rule by voting. They vote for the leaders who govern them. During an election, the side with the majority of votes wins.

1. Write the adjective form of **democracy**. _____

2. Write a synonym for **concept**. _____

3. Write a sentence using the word **democracy**. _____

_____

Almost everyone has a sweet tooth and enjoys a candy snack now and then. Candies differ around the world. Not everyone licks lollipops or munches on chocolate rabbits. Use the Internet, books, or magazines to research various candies around the world. Pick out at least four that you find interesting. Include the name, country, and its ingredients. In the last paragraph of your report, tell if you would like to try any of them. Include illustrations with captions. Proofread your first draft to be sure you have used correct punctuation, capitalization, and grammar.

_____

_____

_____

_____

_____

_____

_____

_____

_____

_____

_____

_____

_____

_____

_____

_____

_____

_____

_____

_____

_____

1. Plot the following coordinates on the coordinate plane. Then, connect the points. What polygon have you created?

   (1, 2) (2, 4) (4, 4) (5, 2)

   _____

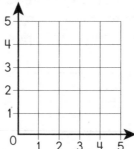

2. 118 × 92 = _____

Day 1

Escaping slaves on the Underground Railroad had to be certain that they could find their way. They needed food and water to make the journey. Conductors helped guide them and provide supplies. One of the most famous Underground Railroad conductors was Harriet Tubman. She had escaped slavery herself. Another famous conductor was Levi Coffin.

1. What part of the Underground Railroad does this paragraph focus on? _____

2. Name two famous conductors. _____

3. What was their job? _____

4. What details did you discover about one of the conductors? _____
   _____

Day 2

1. You are giving a presentation on the lunar cycle. For each phase of the moon, draw an illustration to show what the moon looks like.

waxing crescent	new moon	full moon	waxing gibbous
waning gibbous	waning crescent	first quarter	third quarter

Day 3

Use the clues to write the names of each fruit seller's booth in the correct square.

1. Tony sells apples in the northwest booth.

2. Dawn sells pineapples directly south of Jake's booth.

3. Jake sells oranges directly east of Tony's booth.

4. Shay sells oranges southwest of Jake's booth.

Day 4

Imagine a conversation between the earth, the sun, and the moon about the time of an eclipse. What do you think they would say to each other? Write a dialogue between the earth, the sun, and the moon. Give them personalities! When you have finished, make two copies. Ask two students to join you in reading the three parts. Then, make changes if necessary.

_____

_____

_____

_____

_____

_____

_____

_____

_____

_____

_____

_____

_____

_____

_____

_____

_____

_____

_____

_____

_____

_____

_____

_____

_____

Day 1

1. $\dfrac{3}{6} \times 90 =$ _____

2. Find the volume of the cube.

   _____ cubic inches

   7 in.

3. $486 \times 86 =$ _____

4. Round 11.83 to the nearest whole number.

   _____

Day 2

Use proofreading marks to correct the capitalization errors.
1. does grandpa get the *chicago sun-times* or the *chicago tribune*?

Draw a line under the complete predicate. Circle the predicate verb.
2. The clerk examined the jacket carefully.

Add quotation marks, capitalization, underlines, and punctuation where necessary.
3. Look out screamed Andrew

Circle the correct words in the sentence.
4. Fiona (scent/sent) her (aunt/ant) a birthday card.

Day 3

1. Write the name of each solar system body.

A. _____   B. _____   C. _____   D. _____

2. What is the difference between an asteroid and a meteoroid?

   _____

Day 4

The Great Lakes, located in North America, are the largest bodies of fresh water in the world.

1. Which lake is the largest?

   _____

2. The Great Lakes are between which two countries?

   _____

3. Which Great Lake is the only lake entirely in the United States?

   _____

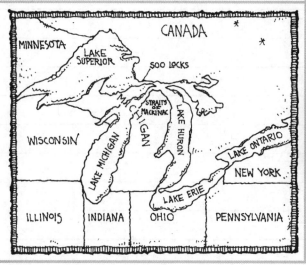

Imagine that your family is camping on the shore of Lake Michigan. Your tent is pitched in the woods about 200 feet (61m) from shore. You just finished a dinner of fried fish caught from the lake. It had been a long, fun day. The whole family was tired except you. They crawled into the tent to sleep. You stayed out by the campfire. All of a sudden, you hear a shuffling sound, twigs crackling, and leaves stirring. What do you do next? Write a story to answer the question. Include your thoughts and decisions. Use dialogue to convey interaction with your family.

_____

_____

_____

_____

_____

_____

_____

_____

_____

_____

_____

_____

_____

_____

_____

_____

_____

_____

_____

_____

_____

_____

_____

_____

Name_____

1. Is a square a rhombus? Explain.

   _____

2. 480 ÷ 8 = _____

3. Write <, >, or = to make the statement true.

   5.632 ◯ 56.32

4. $\frac{3}{5} \times 15 =$ _____

The Aboriginal people in Australia are hunters and gatherers. They are also skilled artists. They have been painting and carving rocks for thousands of years. The paintings are found mostly in caves throughout central Australia. The oldest paintings that have been discovered are about 30,000 years old.

1. Where do Aborigines live? _____

2. What details does the paragraph tell you about them? _____

3. Aborigines are the original dwellers of Australia. What group do they compare with in the United States? _____

You feel hot and have a headache. You wonder if you have a fever. You walk to the medicine cabinet to get a thermometer. Then, you place it in your ear. This kind of thermometer measures the heat, in the form of infrared radiation, coming from your eardrum. Forehead thermometers use this technology as well. Thermometers have come a long way from the breakable glass thermometers filled with toxic mercury.

1. How has engineering improved thermometers? Cite evidence from the passage.

   _____

   _____

A **region** is a part of a country that is different from other parts in some ways. It is usually a large geographic area that has similar features. A region can be defined by geographic features such as wildlife, landforms, or climate. Sometimes a common language, religion, or government defines a region. The continental United States is divided into five basic regions: the West, Southwest, Midwest, Southeast, and Northeast.

1. Define the word **region** in your own words.

   _____

   _____

2. In what region do you live? _____

Name_____

Many careers require the use of mathematics. Some examples of careers that involve mathematics regularly include engineer, fashion designer, chef, and math teacher. Can you think of any others? Use the Internet or books to find other careers that require mathematics. Then, choose one. Write a report about this career choice, including the ways in which mathematics is used on the job. Share your report with a friend.

_____

_____

_____

_____

_____

_____

_____

_____

_____

_____

_____

_____

_____

_____

_____

_____

_____

_____

_____

_____

_____

_____

_____

_____

5.RI.1, 5.RI.4, 5.RI.10, 5.RF.4, 5.W.2, 5.NBT.A.3, 5.NBT.B.6, 5.NF.B.4, 5.G.B.3

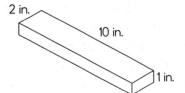

Day 1

1. Find the volume of the rectangular prism.

   _____

2 in.

10 in.

1 in.

2. Round 5.749 to the nearest hundredth.

   _____

3. $7.9 \times 10^5 =$ _____

4. $\frac{3}{8} \times 40 =$ _____

Day 2

Each year, the citizens of the United States **celebrate** two holidays to remember men and women who fought in wars to preserve our freedom. Memorial Day is celebrated on the last Monday in May, and Veterans Day is celebrated on November 11.

1. Which word in this paragraph has a silent consonant pair? _____

2. Circle the synonym for **celebrate** as it is used here: **party** or **observe**.

3. Underline the topic sentence.

4. Which holiday has a date that is relative (the date we observe depends on another factor)? _____

Day 3

Use each term in a sentence to show its meaning. Give an example of each.

1. renewable resource _____

   _____

2. nonrenewable resource _____

   _____

3. inexhaustible resource _____

   _____

Day 4

Earth is composed of 29 percent land. The land is divided into seven continents: Africa, Antarctica, Asia, Australia, Europe, North America, and South America. The five oceans cover most of Earth's surface: Arctic Ocean, Atlantic Ocean, Indian Ocean, Pacific Ocean, and Southern, or Antarctic, Ocean.

1. What percent of Earth is land? _____

2. List the continents according to size from largest to smallest. _____

   _____

3. List the five oceans, beginning with the one that is closest to you. _____

   _____

Memorial Day and Veterans Day are two US holidays that celebrate our freedom and the men and women who fought to preserve it. Use books and the Internet to research how these two holidays came to be. Then, write an informative essay that includes four or five sections. Compare and contrast the two holidays. The last section should include your feelings about the two holidays. Provide a list of sources at the bottom of your essay.

_____

_____

_____

_____

_____

_____

_____

_____

_____

_____

_____

_____

_____

_____

_____

_____

_____

_____

_____

_____

_____

_____

_____

_____

_____

Name_____

1. Look at the triangle on the coordinate grid. If it were moved so that its bottom left vertex was coordinate (5, 4), what would its other coordinates be?

   _____

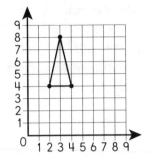

2. (80 – 75) × 2 = _____

Use proofreading marks to correct the capitalization errors.
   1. we're going to an italian restaurant on friday night after we read *strega nona*.

Draw a line under the complete predicate. Circle the predicate verb.
   2. Maddie's dog, Bandit, is a frisky animal.

Add quotation marks, capitalization, underlines, and punctuation where necessary.
   3. Bobbi our class president took charge of today's meeting

Circle the correct words in the sentence.
   4. (Too/To/Two) dollars is a (fare/fair) price.

1. Ozone is a gas found in the stratosphere. How does ozone help people?

   _____

2. Your friend does not understand human impact on the ozone. What examples could you give to help her understand?

   _____

3. What are two effects that will most likely occur if the ozone continues to be destroyed?

   _____

North America is located within the northern and western hemispheres. It is north of South America. It is bordered to the north by the Arctic Ocean, to the east by the Atlantic Ocean, to the southeast by the Gulf of Mexico, and to the west by the Pacific Ocean. In addition to Canada, the United States, and Mexico, this continent includes the Caribbean islands, Central America, and Greenland.

   1. What are the three largest countries in North America? _____

   _____

   2. Which North American countries have you lived in or visited? _____

   _____

Imagine you are the voice of the ozone layer. What would you like to tell people about yourself? Who are you and how do you help the people on Earth? What problems and fears do you have? Talk about how you are changing. Is there a way the people on Earth can help you? Write an informative essay from the viewpoint of the ozone layer to explain these questions. Use books and the Internet to learn more about the ozone layer.

_____
_____
_____
_____
_____
_____
_____
_____
_____
_____
_____
_____
_____
_____
_____
_____
_____
_____
_____
_____
_____
_____
_____
_____

Name_____

1. Round 50.295 to the nearest tenth. _____

2. $\frac{1}{2} \div 21 =$ _____

3. $\frac{5}{6} - \frac{1}{3} =$ _____

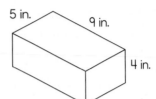
5 in.   9 in.   4 in.

4. Find the volume of the rectangular prism.

   _____

A tarantula has an interesting way to protect itself. It can rub its hind legs together, which causes its stiff leg hairs to fly up in the air. Each tiny hair can cause a hurtful skin or eye wound.

1. Circle all of the words that have a short **i** sound.

2. Which meaning of **wound** is correct here: **wrapped around** or **injury**? _____

3. What details does the writer use to describe tarantula hairs? _____

4. If you looked closely at a tarantula rubbing its hind legs together, what might happen? _____

Tony heard on the news that the city he lives in has a lot of air pollution. He does an experiment in which he spreads petroleum jelly on paper. He puts the paper outside in the morning and then checks it before dinner. The petroleum jelly has a lot of dirt and dust on it.

1. What might have been Tony's hypothesis?

   _____

2. Did Tony's experiment prove his hypothesis? Explain. Then, discuss with a partner.

   _____

North America is full of **amazing** landmarks. Niagara Falls (United States and Canada) is the most famous waterfall in the world. The Grand Canyon (United States) is a national treasure visited by millions of people. Banff National Park (Canada) offers great beauty in summer and winter. Tenochtitlán (Mexico) was built on an island in 1325, and many visit the ruins each year.

1. Write a synonym for **amazing**. _____

2. Compare and contrast any two landmarks. _____

   _____

   _____

Imagine that you are a travel agent. The Espinozas, a very wealthy couple from Brasilia, Brazil, want to travel to beautiful places in North America. They would like to visit as many cities, landmarks, and special places of interest as they can see in four weeks. Use the Internet, books, or magazines to make a list of beautiful and interesting tourist destinations. Then, write a letter to the Espinozas with your recommendations. Remember to place their destinations in a logical sequence of travel, starting and ending with their home airport. Add brief descriptions to your destination choices and separate them with headings. Include a marked map if you wish.

_____

_____

_____

_____

_____

_____

_____

_____

_____

_____

_____

_____

_____

_____

_____

_____

_____

_____

_____

_____

5.RI.1, 5.RI.4, 5.RI.5, 5.RF.3, 5.W.3, 5.W.8, 5.SL.1, 5.L.5, 5.NBT.A.3, 5.NF.A.1, 5.NF.B.7, 5.MD.C.5   CD-104822 • © Carson-Dellosa

1. 1,288 ÷ 2 = _____

2. Anna ran 10 meters, Bill ran 15 meters, and Chloe ran 20 meters. How many centimeters did the three people run in all?

   _____

3. Find the volume of the figure.

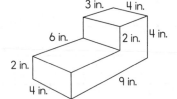

This poem continues through Week 40.
   They call me a three-toed **sloth**, but everyone definitely knows
   When you count them all up, I have 12 gorgeous toes.

1. Is **sloth** pronounced more like **both** or **broth**? _____

2. What word could you use instead of **count**: **add** or **multiply**? _____

3. From whose point of view is this piece written? _____

4. How does that affect how a sloth is described? _____

5. What genre of writing is this? _____

1. What are the three R's for helping the environment? Describe each R word and give examples of how you practice each.

   _____

   _____

   _____

   _____

   _____

Native-born citizens are born in the United States. Others can become native-born citizens if at least one parent is a US citizen. Immigrants can become naturalized citizens if they are age 18, **reside** in the United States for five years, can speak some English, are of good moral character, know American history and government, and take an **oath** of allegiance to the United States and its laws.

1. Write a synonym for **reside**. _____

2. What is an **oath**? _____

3. Name three ways immigrants can become US citizens. _____

   _____

Jesse Owens and Wilma Rudolph are considered two of the fastest runners in the last century. Both of them made track history. There are other famous runners. Use the Internet or books to find out more about famous runners. Choose a famous runner. Write a biography about his life and accomplishments. Be sure to have the correct statistics when you list races and running times.

_____

_____

_____

_____

_____

_____

_____

_____

_____

_____

_____

_____

_____

_____

_____

_____

_____

_____

_____

_____

_____

_____

_____

_____

_____

5.RL.1, 5.RL.4, 5.RL.6, 5.RI.4, 5.RF.3, 5.RF.4, 5.W.2, 5.W.7, 5.L.5, 5.L.6, 5.NBT.B.6, 5.MD.A.1, 5.MD.C.5

Name_____

Day 1

1. 244 ÷ 4 = _____

2. Using the coordinate grid, which ordered pair represents the location of the school?

(_____, _____)

What shape around the school do the four students' houses make? _____

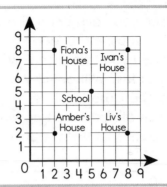

This poem began on Week 37.
I require splendid, tropical rain forests in order to **survive**,
For if it weren't for them, I most certainly wouldn't be alive.

1. What does **survive** mean? _____

2. What fact do you learn about a three-toed sloth in this stanza? _____

3. Who does the pronoun **I** refer to? _____ What about the pronoun **them**?
_____

4. Would a three-toed sloth be found in the deserts of the United States? Explain.
_____

Day 2

Write **true** or **false**. Rewrite any false statements to make them true.

1. _____ There are no drawbacks to alternative energy sources.

2. _____ Some alternative sources, such as wind and solar energy, are inexhaustible.

3. _____ Gasoline is the only substance that can power a car.

4. _____ Geothermal means "earth heat," because it gathers energy from the heat of the earth.

5. _____ Fossil fuels are renewable, but they pollute Earth.

Day 3

Citizens have rights and responsibilities. Their rights are outlined in the US Constitution and Bill of Rights. Some responsibilities are mandatory, such as obeying laws, paying taxes, jury duty, and attending school. Other responsibilities are voluntary such as voting, respecting the rights of others, and volunteering. All of these create a responsible citizen.

1. Write two antonyms that are mentioned in the passage. _____

2. Choose one of the antonyms and write the definition. _____
_____

3. What else might a responsible citizen do? _____
_____
_____

Day 4

Imagine that you have been chosen to volunteer for a week at the Sloth Sanctuary of Costa Rica. Do you like the idea? What do you need to know about Costa Rica before you go? What should you take along? Most importantly, what do you need to know about taking care of baby sloths? Without any research, write two or three paragraphs about your expectations. Then, use the Internet, books, or magazines to learn more about Costa Rica and taking care of sloths. Reread what you wrote before. Revise and add to your writing. When you are satisfied with your report, show it to your teacher. Make changes if needed.

_____
_____
_____
_____
_____
_____
_____
_____
_____
_____
_____
_____
_____
_____
_____
_____
_____
_____
_____
_____
_____
_____
_____
_____

5.RL.1, 5.RL.4, 5.RI.1, 5.RI.4, 5.W.1, 5.W.2, 5.W.5, 5.W.8, 5.W.10, 5.L.5, 5.NBT.B.6, 5.G.A.2

Name_____

Day 1

1. $\frac{3}{4} + \frac{1}{2} =$ _____

2. 757 × 23 = _____

3. Write 74.68 in expanded form.

    _____

4. Find the volume of the figure.

    _____

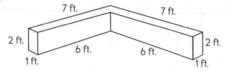

7 ft.   7 ft.

2 ft.   6 ft.   6 ft.   2 ft.

1 ft.   1 ft.

Day 2

This poem began on Week 37.
I'm a downright lazy mammal who's never in a hurry.
My natural coat is brownish green and really very furry.

1. Write the compound word in this stanza. _____

2. What two facts do you learn about a three-toed sloth in this stanza? _____

    _____

3. If you were to see a sloth in its natural environment, what would you expect to see?

    _____

4. Write a simile describing the speed of a sloth. _____

Day 3

Draw a line to match each scientist's name with his or her scientific achievement.

1. Marie Curie

2. Albert Einstein

3. Isaac Newton

4. Lewis Howard Latimer

5. Margaret Mead

A. author of the theory of relativity

B. scientist who discovered the benefits of radium and radioactive therapies

C. anthropologist who studied women's roles in various societies

D. inventor, draftsman, and engineer instrumental in improving lighting

E. author of the three laws of motion

Day 4

In the 18th century, only white, male landowners who were over the age of 21 could vote. Beginning in 1870, a series of Constitutional Amendments and new legislation were passed to extend voting rights to more citizens. To vote in a federal election today, you must be a US citizen, be over the age of 18, and meet certain state requirements.

1. Voting is a right. What responsibility goes with this right? _____

    _____

2. Why is the right to vote important? _____

    _____

Many men and women have done important things in the field of science. Our world would be a different place altogether without their contributions. Jane Goodall studied wild chimpanzees by sitting with them for hours and days. Albert Einstein created the theory of relativity. Isaac Newton developed the theory of gravity. Alexander Graham Bell invented the first telephone. Choose one of these scientists or another scientist. Use the Internet, books, or magazines to learn more about her. Write a report about her life and her discoveries. Use facts and definitions to explain or inform. Write a conclusion that states why you think the world is a better place due to her research.

_____
_____
_____
_____
_____
_____
_____
_____
_____
_____
_____
_____
_____
_____
_____
_____
_____
_____
_____
_____
_____
_____
_____

5.RL.1, 5.RI.1, 5.RF.3, 5.W.2, 5.W.8, 5.NBT.A.3, 5.NF.A.1, 5.MD.C.5

1. $0.20 \div 0.5 =$ _____

2. Plot and connect the points in the order they are listed.

   (2, 5) and (2, 1)

   (2, 5) and (5, 5)

   (2, 3) and (3, 3)

   (2, 1) and (5, 1)   What letter did you make? _____

3. $0.56 \times 10^5 =$ _____

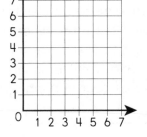

This poem began on Week 37.

I am a lazy animal who sleeps all through the day.

I **feast** only on green plants, and I like it just that way.

1. Is the sloth a carnivore or an herbivore? _____

2. What two facts do you learn about a three-toed sloth in this stanza? _____

   _____

3. What is a synonym for **feast** as it is used in this poem? _____

4. What is the rhyme scheme of this poem?

   A. aa bb cc dd   B. ab ab cd cd   C. free verse

Draw a line to match the name of each science profession with its definition.

1. audiologist	A.	works with Earth's atmosphere and everything in it
2. gemologist	B.	identifies and evaluates stones and minerals
3. physiologist	C.	prepares and dispenses medicines
4. pharmacist	D.	diagnoses and treats hearing loss and imbalance problems
5. horticulturist	E.	studies the chemical, mechanical, and physical makeup of organisms
6. meteorologist	F.	cultivates fruits, flowers, and other plants

---

Everyone in the world lives by rules. If there were no rules or laws, everyone would do what they wanted to do regardless of how it might affect others. Imagine if you worked all day and needed to get a good night's sleep, but your neighbor wanted to play loud music all night. You would have a right to **complain** because most communities have a "disturbing the **peace**" law.

1. Write a synonym for **complain**. _____

2. Write an antonym for **peace**. _____

3. What are other nuisances that could be prevented with a "disturbing the peace" law? _____

Rules are important for many reasons. They are part of everyday life. We are bound by rules at home, in school, on the job, and in public places. Rules are guidelines to help people understand what is expected of them. But, there is a maxim that says, "Know when to break the rules." Are there times when breaking a rule is the right thing to do? Has this ever happened to you? Give this idea some thought. Write an essay that is at least two pages in length. Give reasons to support your opinions. Then, exchange essays with another student and discuss your varying opinions. Make changes if needed.

_____

_____

_____

_____

_____

_____

_____

_____

_____

_____

_____

_____

_____

_____

_____

_____

_____

_____

_____

_____

_____

_____

_____

5.RL.1, 5.RL.4, 5.RI.1, 5.RF.4, 5.W.1, 5.W.5, 5.W.8, 5.L.4, 5.L.5, 5.NBT.A.2, 5.NBT.B.7, 5.G.A.2 CD-104822 • © Carson-Dellosa